THE SCOURGE OF VINYL CAR SEATS

18/29

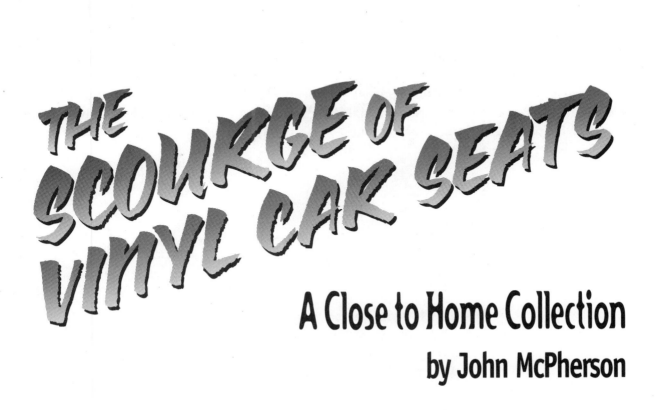

THE SCOURGE OF VINYL CAR SEATS

A Close to Home Collection
by John McPherson

**Andrews McMeel
Publishing**

Kansas City

01 02 03 04 05 BAH 10 9 8 7 6 5 4 3 2 1

ISBN: 0-7407-1845-2

Library of Congress Catalog Card Number: 2001090631

Close to Home may be viewed on the Internet at:
www.uexpress.com

Visit the **Close to Home** Web store at:
www.closetohome.com

E-Mail John McPherson at:
closetohome@compuserve.com

ATTENTION: SCHOOLS AND BUSINESSES

Andrews McMeel books are available at quantity discounts with bulk purchase for educational, business, or sales promotional use. For information, please write to: Special Sales Department, Andrews McMeel Publishing, 4520 Main Street, Kansas City, Missouri 64111.

**To the gang at the Creative Bloc,
creating creative stuff since 1999.**

"Yeah, can you believe it? I cut myself shaving five times this morning! But, hey, enough about my petty problems. Let's get going with Mrs. Felner's cataract surgery."

"This playset cost more than our car, so we came up with a way to share the cost with three of our neighbors."

Hoping to convince management to provide a day-care center, employees at Gormley Industries staged a whine-in.

"It just goes to show ya—almost anything
can be fixed with duct tape!"

"Relax. It's just a can of paint I'm
mixing up in the dryer."

"Brian, this is Mrs. Smithers. From now on,
she'll be chaperoning you when you surf the Net."

"Brad and Wendy would now like to share with you this sculpture, which they created as a symbol of their love and desire to spend as much time together as possible."

"Quit babbling about whether or not it's legal! Just
run to the bank and get 50 dollars in quarters!"

"Just try to remain calm, Art. They can sense fear."

"Great move callling in sick the last two days!
Everyone in your office did a lottery pool yesterday.
They hit the Lotto for $27 million today!"

"Geesh! Check out the mug on
that poor little devil!"

On her flight from New York to Paris,
Paula falls victim to a diaper scalper.

"The landlord won't let us hang any pictures."

"OK, what'd you do with my
beer bottle collection?!"

"How ironic is this? Here I am telling the president
of one of the nation's largest HMOs that the
surgery he needs isn't covered by his insurance!"

Cutting-edge technology for couch potatoes: foot-activated remotes.

"This'll just take a second. It was my husband's last request."

"Watkins! Your blatant disregard for casual day is destroying morale around here! Either you change into these clothes now, or we'll find a position for you down in the mail room!"

"Here's an interesting piece of trivia. Since the baby was born, I've had 957 hours of sleep. You've had 1,429."

"Joyce, get that idiot who gave the
stress-management seminar on the phone!"

"... and when a blade of grass grows high enough to break the beam of the electric eye, the power to your son's stereo and computer will be instantly shut off."

"OK, Howard. We'll play two more rounds using the training clubs, and, if all goes well, you'll play your first solo round on **Wednesday**."

"It's new. It's called 'The Days Remaining Until School Starts Channel.'"

"Don't worry, Mr. Wincott. I'll have that wisdom tooth out of there in no time!"

New technology for parents.

"OK, Mr. Cynic! Twenty-two years and four kids
later, it still fits! Pay up!"

"Mr. Ginsler, for the fifth time, when I get to the part where you can object to the marriage, I will let you know!"

"Say, do you folks love a good mystery?
If so, this is the house for you!"

"So you don't like it. Big deal! You think
I like spending two hours every day
helping you look for your car keys?!"

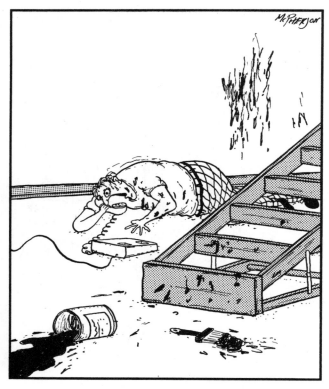

**"For cryin' out loud, you idiot. I'm serious!
I really have fallen and I can't get up!"**

"Didn't anybody tell you? Fridays are casual day in the O.R."

"Dr. Johnson will be ready for you in just a minute."

The staff at Happy Hearts Day Care had its own unique way of penalizing parents who were late picking up their kids.

"Hey, Virgil, come here! Check out the
cheesy-looking toupee collection
El Dorko there is packing!"

"It's U.L. approved, plus it's guaranteed
for up to 50,000 volts!"

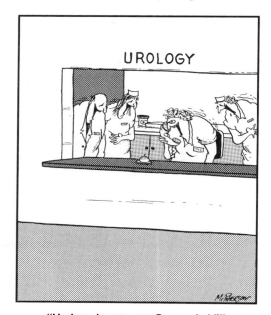

"Urology department. Can you hold?"

Studies have revealed that 72 percent of all
household injuries are caused by adults trying
to step over toddler safety gates.

"I told you folks over the phone that it's
an efficiency apartment."

"My, Helen, that certainly was
a strong contraction!"

"Here are the keys. The tank is full.
You have a great time tonight, big guy!"

Doug and Romney get fired.

"You'll be happy to know that the plane landed safely. I *said*, the plane landed safely. *Hello*?!"

"For an additional one dollar per ticket, would you like to buy disability insurance?"

"OK, now here's *your* horoscope! 'Romance and adventure are yours for the taking! Today's the day to tackle that big project you've been dying to get at.'"

"Is that thing locked up again? You need to smack the side of the CPU while simultaneously hitting the 'T' key as fast as possible."

"Let me get this straight. You're going to build us a wraparound front porch using skills gleaned solely from watching old episodes of 'Home Improvement'?"

"That mower comes with a case of your favorite beverage."

Freak shows for parents.

"One, it's at *least* three miles away! Two, there's only a 40 percent chance that it'll come this way. Three, I'm two under par through 12 holes!"

"It's called Pompeii Disease. It's not serious, but I suggest you wear old clothes for the next couple of weeks."

"Would it kill you to spend 15 bucks on a lawn sprinkler?!"

"The cable company added 'The Croquet Channel,' 'The Hygiene Channel,' and 'The Potato Network.' They raised their rates $15."

"For the last 45 minutes he'd been raving about what incredible TV reception we were getting, and then 'Wham!'"

"Ma'am, I'm new on the job today. Could you take a photo of your husband and me as I issue my very first speeding ticket?"

"OK, Vern! Danny and I are going to flush the roaches toward you!
Get ready to dance 'La Cucaracha'!"

"I hope you don't mind if we stop in here until that rain lets up."

"Well, what'd you expect?! I've been telling you for two years that we need health insurance!"

In their never-ending quest to cut overhead costs, many companies are turning to the new micro-cubicles.

The affordable and increasingly popular face-lift clip.

"Booth No. 1 will be available in about seven minutes. I'm cooking a TV dinner in there."

"OK, today we test your reflexes."

49

"How do you feel about alternative medicine?"

"Isn't that pop-up book just the cutest thing?"

Every September, school buses everywhere incur millions of dollars of damage by souvenir-scavenging parents of kindergartners.

"Well, that pretty much wipes out my tips for the evening."

"OK, Captain Anxiety. I took some Polaroids before we left. Exhibit A: the stove with all burners clearly in the 'off' position. Exhibit B: the back door with it's deadbolt latched. Exhibit C: my curling iron unplugged ..."

Relying on his vast CD collection, manager Walt Friboski liked to provide an appropriate soundtrack when he gave performance reviews.

"Oh, I see! So it's *my* fault that a butterfly darted in front of the car and I had to slam on the brakes, is that it?!"

"Well, how do you like my new system for making sure
my tools get returned?"

"OK, free HBO! Come to Papa!"

"Ma'am would you mind wearing this for about 10 minutes? We're going to play a little prank on the gentleman sleeping in the seat in front of you!"

"The idea gave me the creeps at first, but when Frank showed me the numbers I had to admit that selling burial plots in our yard is a great way to put the kids through college."

"I'm curious. Why is this technique called the Holyfield Maneuver?"

"Tell me again how much money we're saving by cutting our own firewood!"

With baby-sitters in short supply, the
Cranstons shrewdly installed Mr. Eye®.

Chuck considered the interview to be over after
the job applicant consulted her Magic Eight Ball®
to answer three consecutive questions.

Denise is able to avert yet another disaster
thanks to her Toddler Retrieval System.

"It's the latest version of the stress test. We'll monitor your heart rate as you try to feed these seven hungry babies with just one bottle."

"Gina, before you make the biggest mistake of your life, I want you to meet Esther Baumgarten's son, Rudy. Rudy is assistant manager of Pizza Baron, *and* he plays the clarinet!"

Though they hadn't even stepped inside yet, veteran real estate agent Clair Gelt knew the sale was in the bag.

"Will you shut up about how great the fishing is?!"

Thanks to the innovative labs of teacher Herb Krenley, physics quickly became Westvale High's most popular course.

**By the time he turned thirteen, Bryan was starting
to see through his father's little scam.**

Todd's relationship with management improved
dramatically once he started bringing his new
pet to work.

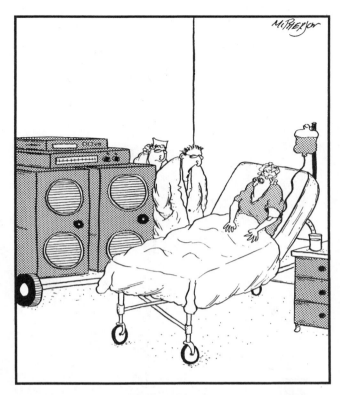

"We're going to try to disintegrate the kidney
stone with a three-hour barrage of music
by the rock band Pearl Jam."

"Well, hon, it took $1,400 and 57 hours of hard labor, but we did it! I can't wait to see the looks on the kids' faces!"

"Oh, that. I got it from the Healthy Lifestyles catalog. It automatically dispenses a dab of sunscreen anytime someone leaves the house."

Jason proves that he wasn't lying about the fate of his homework.

Tiger Woods: the early months.

Trish realizes she has just entered into a lifetime with a chronic do-it-yourselfer.

"It's so vintage Ray! When he got a riding mower, he had to have the one with the built-in TV and back massager. When we picked out a dog, he tested them all to see which one had the highest IQ."

"Serenity Noelle! The name we want on the birth certificate is Serenity Noelle Wagner! Write it down! *Write it down, I said!*"

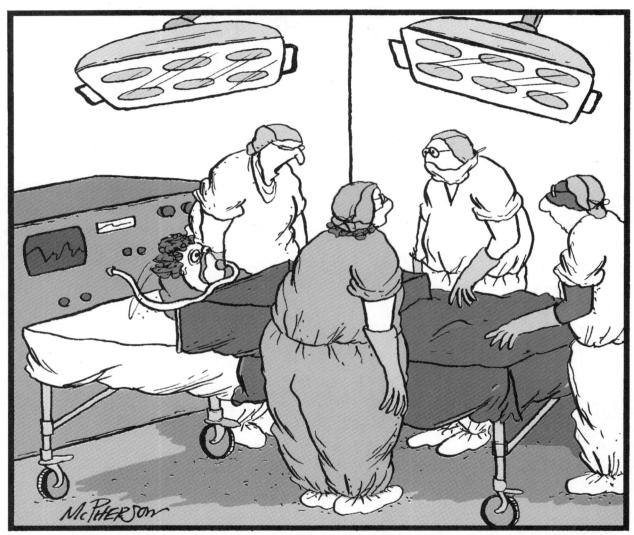

"And remember this time, Bobby! Number each item as it comes out so we're sure it goes back in the right order!"

Evolving through centuries of picking up table scraps, the Hoover Hound has come to play an important role in many households.

"Mr. Hopkins! We're having a bit of trouble with the new laser printer."

As soon as they got onto the bus, Roger and Glenda had an unshakable sense of foreboding.

Bizarre though it was, the Merkles had stumbled onto a system for picking stocks that netted them $11,761 in just five months.

"I see one! I see a rest room! There's a woman coming out ... it looks clean in there ... no sign of flies ..."

"OK, folks! It's time to find out which of these lovely, single gals will be the lucky one to catch the bouquet!"

"Knock it off, Carlos! Remember, we agreed that
Isabelle would choose her own day-care provider."

"Look at that, everyone! Annette was able to walk right past the computer *even though she knows* there are 27 e-mails waiting for her!"

"You heard me, Mendrick! No hands or feet allowed!"

"Well, Mr. Floor-It-We-Can-Make-It, do you *still* want me to rush home so you don't miss the Packers game?"

"It's constructed out of the same soundproofing
material that **NASA** uses on the space shuttle,
and it's hypoallergenic."

"First, the 900-square-foot heated tree fort. Then the fully operational backyard planetarium. And now this. It's all a well-orchestrated plot to make us look like the world's lousiest parents."

"I'm tellin' ya! Ever since you rigged up that
smoke machine under the table, I just
can't *wait* to get to work every day!"

"Eh, eh, eh! You know the rules!
No bugging Mom at work!"

"1,200 hits a day?! Big deal! My Web
site averages 18,000 hits a day!"

Through well-planned provocation, Vince was able
to harvest enough toilet paper during Halloween
to keep the family supplied for an entire year.

"The doctor says she'll grow into her tongue."

Whenever one of his daughters returned from a date, Mr. Shelburne would carefully dust her for fingerprints.

"Mix five grams of potassium nitrate with three milliliters of
sodium chloride, add a dab of nail polish, and then
rub it on your stomach."

"With your gingivitis flaring up again, I figured it was a
good idea to invest in a power flosser."

Barry does his trick of clenching all his muscles at once and getting his I.V. bag to expand.

With just three days until Halloween, the kids of Maple Avenue had their surveillance teams in place.

The fake rubber leg that Diane kept in her purse livened up many a first date.

After debuting its new weather format, TV 52's ratings soared to No. 1.

"When I was a kid, we had to get up, walk clear across the room, and turn a dial on the TV whenever we wanted to change the channel."

Before giving out candy, the Gernsteads required that trick-or-treaters first watch a short video on dental care.

"Well, there's a good one to know about. 'Stereo ... receiver ... needs ... to be ... moved up ... higher.'"

"Oooooh, this is exciting! Our first practical application for the Internet! OK, should I do a search under 'pythons,' 'snakes' or 'suffocation'?"

"Bill's away for two weeks, and he made me swear not to let the baby take her first steps until he's home to see the big event."

"The face-lifting technique we'll be performing on you is somewhat controversial. So just to be on the safe side, we want to try it on this lab rat first."

The year the SAT creators decided to mess with students' minds.

"I knew we were in trouble the second he yelled that old 'Look, Ma, no hands!' line."

Thanks to their new aromatic spray bottles, the Girl Scouts experienced a 147 percent increase in cookie sales.

"We should have gotten off the plane the second we overheard the pilot say he's an ex-Blue Angel."

"One minute I was checking out Web sites on spaying and neutering pets, the next minute ..."

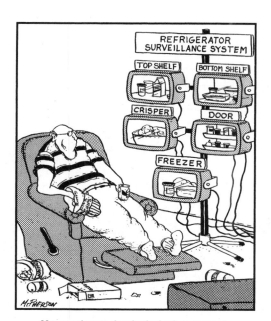

Yet another technological advancement for couch potatoes.

Alex Trebek's secret moonlighting job.

Having successfully completed her shopping
without a major tantrum, Linda now had to
run the harrowing gauntlet of toy and
candy dispensers.

"Well now! Maybe the next time I tell you that the
car is making a funny rattling noise, I won't get
one of your condescending smirks!"

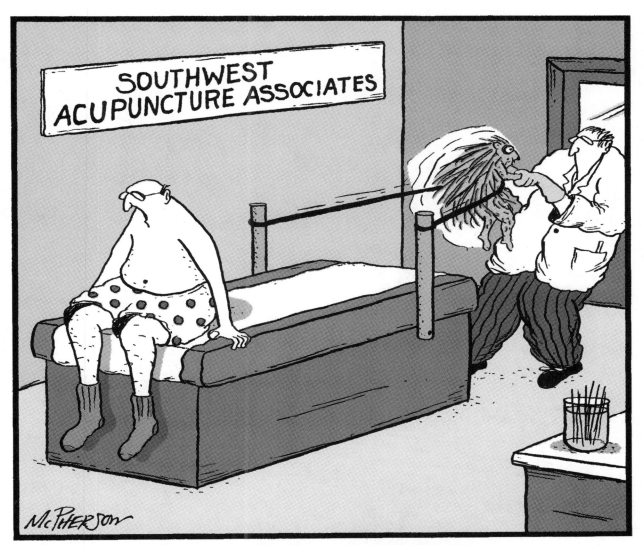

"A new technique? Hey, whatever. I'll try
anything to get rid of this killer headache."

"Whoa, hold up, Bert! What do we have here in the back seat?! A little book titled *How to Sweet-Talk Your Way out of Any Speeding Ticket!*"

"There are two divergent opinions on how best to treat you. I'm convinced you need a triple bypass. Your HMO says all you need to do it rub this $14 tube of salve on your chest."

Mr. Hagy couldn't resist pulling out his remote-control frog at least once a year.

Knowing that her manager would never allow her to leave early to watch her son's soccer game, Wendy hires a body double.

The Gilmonts play a tension-filled game
of chore poker.

"Oh, yeah, now I remember. The roofing contractor
left a message saying you should call him ASAP."

"Well, at last we have a volunteer to do the oral report on quantum physics."

"Yeah, well, where's Kathie Lee now?!"

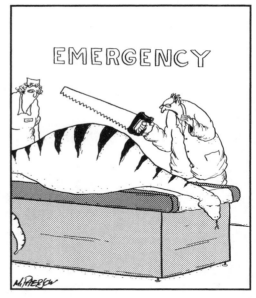

"OK, Mr. Morris. I need to have you
scoot as far to your left as possible."

"Isn't genetic engineering amazing? Two years
ago who would have even imagined
such a thing as a Turkipede?!"

With the electricity out and their emergency
generator able to power only the stove or
the TV, tensions in the Normont household
were at a fevered pitch.

104

"Aw, come on, Mr. Sinclair! Don't be such a gloomy Gus!
A little friendly athletic competition will do wonders
for your spirits! I'll be your cheerleader!"

Scandal rocks the whale-watching industry.

"Guess how many stitches you've got, within three, and we'll take 10 percent off your bill!"

"Cosgrove, get back here!"

"Well I'll be! Sheila, it's *another* electronic listening device! Santa's helpers must have bugged our house to see who's being naughty or nice!"

While Jack kept the Watkinses distracted in the kitchen, Muffy combed their house for their secret black book of baby-sitters.

"Sorry about this, Carol. I was positive that the door at the back of the theater was an exit."

**Having passed the state's driver exam, Tammy now
had to pass her father's grueling 12-part version.**

"Sorry, but the life preserver is required by our insurance company."

Hoping to break out of their traditional mold, the Mormon Tabernacle Choir performs the barking dogs version of "Jingle Bells."

"Oh, that? I thought I told you. *Dateline NBC* is going to feature us in a segment titled 'Working Couples: Who Does the Brunt of the Housework?'"

"Will you knock it off with the *Chicken Soup for the Soul* excerpts!"

"Before we waste your time and mine, let's see if you can fit through this opening."

Hoping to catch some discreet Zees during the film in biology, Brian brings his head-prop and plastic eyeballs.

CHICKEN SOUP

"OK, Bobby! You can open your eyes now!"

Spotting some unexpected visitors coming up the walk, the Hadleys activated their hidden clean living room.

"No, the color of that tree clashes with Dad's chair. Let's head up the hill to that grove of Scotch pines and see if there are any suitable trees there."

In a rare display of emotion, gym teacher Art Mankowski succumbs to the spirit of Christmas.

"You still want us to change the oil?"

**"Come on! Where's your sense of humor?
All I'm going to do is stroll her
through the mall!"**

"Are you gonna whine, or are you gonna let me fix your back?!"

"I'm tellin' ya, Louise, that's the only thing that keeps me from going insane on rainy days."

"It's very unlikely that you'll ever need to use them, but
if that red light comes on, start pedaling like crazy."

"Uh, yeah, Homework Help Line? I need to have you explain
the quadratic equation in roughly the amount of time
it takes to get a cup of coffee."

"See, you thought it was real! I tell ya,
hologram Christmas trees are the way to go!"

"We ran into some complications
with your appendectomy."

"Mrs. Killigrew, I'm sure I explained it to you over the phone. It emits a crippling, high-pitched squeal that *only thieves can hear*. Now if you'll just sign at the bottom ..."

"Before Ramona says 'I do,' Phil, she'd like you to inspect this bathroom scene and make whatever corrections you feel are needed."

"Well, I'm sorry, but if you don't have a
receipt for the pacemaker there's
not much we can do for you."

Only a veteran mom can master the
art of hands-free stroller unfolding.

Carol sensed that the romance was slowly slipping from their marriage.

"We tried flea dips, powders, and sprays. But our vet finally convinced us that organic flea treatment was the way to go."

"We've already had endorsement offers
from three shampoo companies."

"OK, ma'am, here's how our Super Value tug-of-war works!
You two battle it out for 60 seconds, and wherever the
value arrow winds up is the price you walk away with!"

"Well, no wonder! The tubes were switched!
This thing's been running in reverse."

Metal-shop teacher Hank Borgner prided
himself in his back-to-basics curriculum.

The new kinder, gentler IRS.

"Well, we had her declawed but started feeling guilty that she couldn't climb trees any longer. And then Frank saw this ad in the back of *Popular Mechanics* ..."

"Oh, calm down, dear! No one's looking! Just let me tweeze these little hairs you've got, so David doesn't think he's marrying Groucho Marx."

Another marketing success for the Postal Service.

"Oh, come on. Don't be such a grouch! The kids worked so hard on it, and you'll be able to see where you're driving just fine."

"Hey, I've had it with getting them in and out of winter clothes. This new flexible foam insulation goes on quickly and peels right off."

"Holy cow! *Now* we've got a pulse!"

Life with a chronic article-clipper.

"Hey, the sooner he learns to crawl, the sooner he'll learn to walk. The sooner he learns to walk, the sooner he can mow the lawn."

"If you want my opinion, this is all just a scam to get us to fork over $75 for graduation gown rentals!"

"OK, fine. So now you never have to shovel the
driveway again. Explain to me how you're going
to keep the paper boy from catching on fire."

Essential training for expectant parents.

At the funeral of the inventor
of the jack-in-the-box.

"The salesman told me he caught 23 northern
pikes in less than an hour while swimming
in a pair of these."

"And now, Dr. Johnson is going to juggle four
syringes of Novocain while he simultaneously injects
you with a fifth one!"

A revolutionary breakthrough in driver education
technology: Nerf cars.

"Your carpal tunnel syndrome should clear up in two weeks, plus you'll burn 500 calories an hour."

"OK, there! I don't want to hear anyone whining about how long it takes for the water to get hot!"

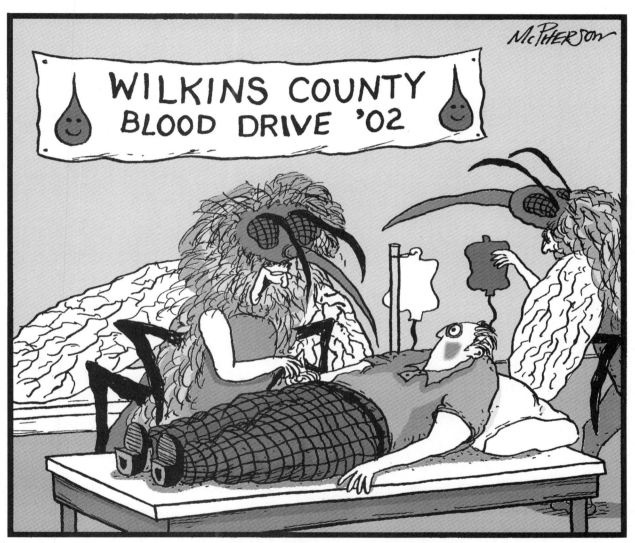

"It's just a way of maintaining a sense of humor around here.
Now if you'll just clench your fist ..."